BE WELL,
DETROIT

BE WELL, DETROIT

Empowering a city lost to

* the unrest in the 60's, created by the racial inequalities in America
* the busing experiment in the name of equal education that disrupted the neighborhoods
* drug use and abuse
* poverty, a complex issue with many causes
* a violent segment of the population
* stealing cars, sometimes at gun point
* a culture that enables girls and women to have children without a plan to support them emotionally or financially

Dana Coyne

authorHOUSE®

AuthorHouse™ LLC
1663 Liberty Drive
Bloomington, IN 47403
www.authorhouse.com
Phone: 1-800-839-8640

Published by AuthorHouse   08/08/2013

ISBN: 978-1-4817-5740-9 (sc)
ISBN: 978-1-4817-5998-4 (e)

Library of Congress Control Number: 2013909886

This book is printed on acid-free paper.

The views expressed in this work are solely those of the author and do not necessarily reflect the views of the publisher, and the publisher hereby disclaims any responsibility for them.

It is time.

CONTENTS

For Peace And Prosperity

Over the past three decades I have watched this city gradually disappear. Many people, who worked in Detroit, held on to living in Detroit into the 1980's. Some people have stayed and some have moved in during those three decades. Many have left and the city has been disappearing. Since I first began writing down my ideas for transforming Detroit, lots of changes have taken place. There are people and businesses that are coming back or coming for the first time. They want to be a part of the new, really great Detroit!

People want to come to Detroit. They want to play in the city. It's just that one needs to watch their back so closely, that people are deterred. They don't want to be accosted at gun point for their vehicle and they don't want to come up against a drug addict who wants to steal from them and may harm them in the process. This city will be back and be great again, when it is healed. It is the healing process that I speak of here, now. It is time to heal Detroit.

I speak of healing by way of education.

There was a time when the public schools did a great job of educating nearly all of Detroit's students. There are some things that need to be put into place in order for that to be the case again. When the public schools have leadership with integrity, wisdom and the tools necessary to deal with the problems that Detroit has, we will succeed. The leaders will look at what is missing and have some clarity about what needs to be put in place in order to transform the public school district into a successful school district. It is then that the city will once again have an opportunity to be successful as well.

A successful school district addresses the needs of its community. When the true needs, the underlying issues are addressed, we will begin the process of healing Detroit.

When it is clearly understood what is needed and we put that in, we will succeed. Detroit will be a destination for world travelers. They will come to see the transformation. They will smile, they will have joy in their hearts, they will see the true peace that comes with being healed, being responsible and living into the possibility that living is. It is in The Lord's Prayer that we pray, "Thy Kingdom come, Thy Will be done, on Earth as it is in Heaven." To live life as God intended and having life be Heaven on Earth, will come with trust in God and living as God requests that we live our lives. It is through love, patience and understanding that we will thrive.

The educational needs of many of the students in the city of Detroit go far beyond reading and math. A strong curriculum that addresses the self esteem of each student will transform this district. When all of our children see the greatness in themselves, when they see who they really can be, when they are given the opportunity to dream and use their imaginations to invent their lives, they will be able to rise above the issues that have been holding generations of families back from accomplishing great success along with being truly peaceful and happy. Throughout the years we have celebrated many success stories! It is time for many more.

I look forward to the day that Detroit is thriving, new neighborhoods are springing up and the public schools are once again doing an excellent job at educating all of the children in Detroit.

Why? For the love of a city that once was thriving and prosperous, filled with people

who were happy and satisfied, living the
American dream. For that to be, again. For
pleasure and joy. For shopping and fun and
games. For smiles and peace.

Who Is Detroit?

Detroit is a big Midwestern city that has been disappearing because of the poverty, drug use, violence and a school district that has not addressed the needs of the community.

Detroit is the Motor City, Motown, the Home of the Detroit Tigers, the Detroit Lions, the Detroit Red Wings and maybe once again the Detroit Pistons. Detroit has a cultural center with world class museums and entertainment. Detroit is rich with incredible architecture and art! Detroit is Eastern Market. Detroit is great restaurants and bars. Detroit is a city on the beautiful Detroit River. Detroit is a city in the fabulous state of Michigan! Detroit is a variety of neighborhood communities that thrive peacefully with residents who are respectfully appreciative of one another. Detroit is Mexican Village and Greektown and the eastside and the westside and Woodward Avenue. You can get to Canada by way of the Tunnel, the Ambassador Bridge or on a boat from Detroit. As the hub for many diversified cities and communities in southeast Michigan, Detroit brings people together for work and play. There are colleges and universities, lots of places to learn things and take kids to learn things, too!

Detroit is a city who has fallen apart because of the deeply rooted issues that have not been addressed and dealt with for decades. Parts of her are beat up, trashed up, broken down and have not been tended to for decades. It is sad to drive through parts of Detroit and see just how badly she has fallen down.

Detroit is also a city on her way back. Lots of people are working on having Detroit be great again. Many of the old ways that have not worked are beginning to change! Lots of people are believers! It is truly heartening that people are rallying to create Detroit to be great again!

Detroit is the big city that suburbanites delight in coming to for special events that include, sports and dinner and culture. Gathering with friends in the big city is enjoyable. People who live in Detroit like to live in a city that is happening and has visitors that contribute to its economy and bustle!

Detroit is Belle Isle and other parks, many of them waiting for tender loving care. Detroit could be such a beautiful city, especially considering that she is positioned on the Detroit River. It is time that we utilize the river to its fullest extent in Detroit.

Detroit is new business along with some of the old business. She is being reinvented. There are teams of people planning a future Detroit and let me tell you, the plans are absolutely incredible!

Detroit is not a shopping Mecca, except for the strip malls, the liquor stores, the phone and the dollar stores, and the gas stations. When the problems associated with crime became rampant, the downtown shopping district could not be maintained any longer. When Detroit is healed we can build up our shopping district again. Things are starting to happen downtown. A central location for some really great shopping is part of what makes a city great.

Detroit is getting ready for all the pieces to come together, to thrive and be joyful. Prosperity and peace for all of Detroit will be here soon. You are invited to believe and if you see the opportunity to contribute and make a difference, go for it, make a difference!

How Do We Create The Peace . . . .

Eliminate The Violence . . . .
Eliminate The Automobile Stealing . . . .
Eliminate The Problems Associated With Drugs . . . .
Eliminate The Killing Or Harming Of People?

We create a public educational system that is set up to win and educate people such that they can choose responsibility.

Presently, this is not occurring in many of the public schools. When one cannot read and/or has self esteem issues, choosing responsibility for some is not an option. Choosing to have a baby is what comes up, a lot. Choosing to do drugs comes up. Illegal drugs are a serious problem in Detroit. Much of the crime in Detroit is drug related. Ultimately those choices frequently lead directly to poverty and a struggle, then the cycle repeats itself. Often times, all of that leads to absentee parents, with grandparents

8

now raising the next generation and that may not be an ideal situation.

There is lots of struggling in the city of Detroit. Poverty, depression, drug use, having to use a bus as transportation in a city with so much crime it can be fearful and on a bus system that can be difficult to maneuver from location to location due to a shrinking city all contribute to the struggling.

Education, Education, Education! That is how we will transform this city. Along with teaching reading, math and science we need to focus on the issues at hand; generational poverty, children having children, violence and low self esteem being such that a great life is not part of the belief system for many. These issues can be addressed in mandatory Life Skills or Home and Family Living type courses that would include, Health and Well Being, Financial Responsibility, Career Awareness and Guidance, Parenting Courses and a Human Sexuality Program that is Abstinence Based.

Education! Education! Education!

Focus on:

Health and Well Being

Financial Responsibility

Career Awareness and Guidance

Parenting Courses

Abstinence Based Human Sexuality Curriculum

Who Is This Book For?

This book is for those who would like to see Detroit (or any city for that matter) be fabulous, vibrant, fun and safe again.

This book is for people who are curious about what has gone on in this city to contribute to it's falling apart, it's disappearing, the poverty and the crime. This book is for people who want to know what could be put in place that would change the course of continued struggle, poverty and crime to a course of peace, prosperity and joy for all.

This book is for people who are ready to be a part of the solution.

This book is for people who have not quite seen the possibility of Detroit being a peaceful, beautiful and a vibrant place. Many doubt that it is possible. They resist the bold speaking that Detroit will be safe and great again. They have not yet taken the stand that peace, prosperity and joy are within our grasp. The doubters are invited to believe that when the school district has a wise plan that addresses the needs of her constituents and the plan is carried out with affinity and boldness, it will be possible to transform this city by way of the educational system.

This book is for people who want some guidance as to what they might have to offer up in the way of volunteerism and contribution. This book is to motivate people to see that they are the change agents and they can be a part of the solution.

There are many opportunities for people to contribute to the healing, the well being of Detroit. Go online and check out the websites, there is a place for everyone to contribute. You are invited to explore and connect with what will create satisfaction for you and take the action needed to be satisfied.

More specifically this book addresses the public school system and what is presently missing, that is contributing to Detroit not being peaceful and prosperous. When things are missing and the business at hand is not being taken care of, things tend to fall apart and disappear. That is what has happened to Detroit. Some changes need to take place. When the changes are in place, we will see the disease and the underlying causes dissipate and the transformation will take place.

Do You Want To Be A Part Of The Solution?

If so, read on, look for your opportunity and take action, make something happen. You are invited to be a part of creating some joy and responsibility.

Who are you, really? We know that contributing is satisfying. There are people waiting to plant a tree with you! You could assist with athletics. Maybe you like cleaning or sprucing up a neighborhood or a park, you get to choose and take satisfaction in your contribution. Gather your friends and brainstorm a project up and have some fun being a part of the solution! Find a school, develop a plan and go see if they like your plan or ask them what they need and see if you can work together on creating a difference making project. Join in with the experienced, work with and learn from them.

Life happens out of the conversations that we are. One day Detroit will be an incredible city again. I see a city beyond anything that we have seen before in a city. Peacefulness, beauty, recreation, joy, prosperity, order, excitement, pleasure, fitness, and well being that are all working together synchronistically

to create healthy people and a healthy
economy. Maybe we need some billboards
speaking those words, out loud, for everyone to
become enrolled into. If you can see it, enroll
your friends and come play, come work, come
be a part of the transformation. Come be a
part of transforming and creating one of the
greatest city on the planet!

We are in a time of transition. Bad
things may still happen. Pay attention,
do not be blind to the possibility of crime
and destruction happening. With the
transformation of the educational system will
come the lessening of crime and destruction.
Be wise in your choices and locations.

Planning Is Crucial

If we are going to transform this city, the educational system needs a **Plan of Action** that addresses the needs of its constituents.

Over the past three decades simply getting students enrolled on the first day of school has been an issue that has contributed to many of the problems that have created the breakdown of the district and the city. It has been a practice in the city of Detroit for students to show up and register over a period of weeks and that is insanity when it comes to staff distribution, supplies and getting the year started.

In order to get organized in a school, we need to know who will be enrolled into the school. The school needs to know how many teachers are required in order to conduct the business of educating students. In years past there has been a lot of transiency in Detroit. Families do a lot of moving and there are many students who simply do not show up until a week or two or three after the first day of school. Efficiency and effectiveness at the beginning of the school year are not possible under these circumstances.

Mandatory registration of all students in Wayne County must be completed by July 15. Central Offices need time to do the work of placing students in the most appropriate school. With a shrinking city and a shrinking school district there needs to be a **Plan of Action** and it needs to be carried out with integrity and heart and soul. Registration needs to be complete by July 15. Wayne County would be the goal, rather than the City of Detroit, because of the many charter schools and cities that neighbor Detroit who have opened their doors for enrollment. That would greatly assist them as well.

Parents need to be made aware of this **registration due date** and take action. This due date needs to be published on the front of every news publication throughout the county every day, beginning in May and going through July 15. TV and email alerts would be helpful, as well. The parents of every student who was previously enrolled in Wayne County, who doesn't get registered by July 15, will need to be contacted by the school where the child was last enrolled and be asked where they intend to register their child. Parents will be told that they will be notified about where their child(ren) will be attending school as soon as that has been determined.

Parents who fail to register their students by the **registration deadline** need to be required to attend a series of Parenting Workshops, beginning with a workshop on "The Importance of Registering Your Student On Time." When a child is not maintaining a "B" average, having an Attendance problem or behaving "inappropriately," parents must be required to take a series of Parenting Workshops. Most often when a child is having an issue or multiple issues it is the parents who could use the support to assist their child in getting back on track. It is the responsibility of parents to make sure that their children get to school on time each and every day and they support their children in cooperating with teachers and other staff members, as well as getting their work completed. When students are having problems, it is the parents to whom we need to extend support and guidance. Workshops could be that support that would help parents in guiding and nurturing their children toward success and happiness.

Registration of all students in Wayne County must be completed by July 15.

In Detroit, we need to get the map out after Registration and figure out who will go where. First to Register, first to be enrolled at the school that is chosen by the parents. There is only so much room in a class for students. Detroit has been known to have some schools with very low enrollment and small class sizes and at the same time there will be a school across town or around the corner with two times as many children in each classroom. This is unfair to the students and to the teachers who have twice the number of students to teach. Equal and fair is appropriate and contributes to everyone's well being and success. When every school is set up fairly and set up to win, we will eliminate many problems associated with registration in the past. As the city gets her neighborhoods planned and we know where the residential areas will be, we can build neighborhood schools and create communities that revolve around the schools again. Right now we need to work with what we have, a transitioning city.

Part of the planning includes the Curriculum. All schools need to have Art, Physical Education and Music along with the required academics and Computer Courses. Special Subject Teachers often give preps to the Elementary Classroom Teachers; they are a part of the mix and need to be planned for.

When you know your enrollment, you can plan. If you do not, it's simple, ineffectiveness sets in.

Teachers need to come in the week before students show up so that the school year can be planned and calendars can be set. Committees need to meet and preparations need to take place. Teachers need time to get their rooms and plans ready. Books need to be distributed; they need to be in the rooms before the teachers arrive in August. All supplies need to be in the classrooms before the teachers arrive.

Plan! Plan! Plan!

All programs need to be on the calendar. Anything that can be scheduled needs to be scheduled in August. District wide planning needs to take place as well in advance as possible so that when the teachers return, they can work with the district wide calendar and plan for their school's year.

Plan! Plan! Plan!

No kidding!

Yearly Calendars
go home
on the first day of school!

EFFECTIVE PROFESSIONAL DEVELOPMENT
AND TRAINING IS ESSENTIAL

EVERYONE NEEDS TO BE ON THE SAME PAGE

If every staff member who works in any capacity in the public schools is empowered to see what is possible and know that they are part of a team that can accomplish the incredible, the incredible will happen. When people understand their responsibility in the matter and understand that we create life into our speaking, we can make a difference. Until we have a team of people who see incredible possibilities and truly understand that amazing results are actually possible, people will continue to be stuck in, "That'll never happen," or "That's not possible," or "It'll always be that way, pitiful." When everyone on the team begins to see that it is possible to make what has been impossible happen, we will begin to make it happen.

Generating what is possible begins the process. Being bold and confident is a big part of generating incredible results. Being

committed to incredible results is necessary.
Action that aligns with the commitment will
create results. Living into what is possible
will keep the dream alive. We can do this.
Greatness is upon us. When the public schools
have a plan that is set up for success, the staff
will align and we will see results. Up to this
point things have clearly not been set up for
us to win. Many have lost sight of the dream
of being successful. When we have a winning
plan that is laid out for all to see, it will be
possible for the team to believe in incredible
results. Being set up to win must be in place,
or we will be back to failure and frustration
and sadness. There must be a winning plan
in place for people to be able to believe and
live into what is possible. The transformation
will not happen if we keep doing what we
have been doing for decades. Big changes are
necessary or we will continue to be stuck in
a bad place. It is time for peace. It is time for
healing.

Being . . . . .

Being is a state of mind.

If one is being pessimistic,

the results are that, too.

People be that they are right

in their pessimism.

If people shift their thinking

to one of optimism,

and possibilities,

the results shift, too!

Imagine every staff member
who works in the
public schools
having the attitude
that anything is possible.

<u>Just what could be possible?</u>

Be reminded of the quote from
Saint Augustine,

Faith is to believe

what you do not see,

the reward of this Faith

is to see what you believe.

Think about how America got started.
It was made up. We have an opportunity to
make it up here in Detroit. It will take some
people who can think and see big. It will
take each and every staff member to make it
happen. When everyone is looking to create
a successful school district and an incredible
city, we will have a chance to actually make it
happen.

We do need believers. Everyone needs to
be on board. It hasn't been working with a
few believers, everyone needs to see the vision
and believe that it will happen, not only in
their lifetime, soon, real soon, like within
the next 5-10 years we could see a marked
improvement. In 15 to 20 years this city could
be well on her way to being safe, prosperous
and joyful!

Effective Professional and Personal Training for every staff member in the public schools

would include training
that supports people in
transforming their personal lives,
in order for them to become action beings.
Sometimes people tend to be reaction beings
and that contributes to disempowerment
instead of empowerment.

When people develop an understanding
of why people do what they do,
they do not have to react and
create a deeper problem,
they can bring empathy
and the ability to empower
those around them
and create a solution to the problem.
They can bring patience and love and
understanding.

If everyone
who comes into the
public schools
to do any work,
participates in
effective personal training and
development
this city will be transformed
much quicker
than it is on track
to be transformed.
People with an understanding
of human nature
are more able and likely
to empower
every person
around them.

If you think about it, any company or organization must have everyone on board for the company to succeed. If you have a negative person on the staff who infects the organization, progress gets delayed and problems occur.

When we have a team of people with an understanding of human nature and are clear that life is for the inventing, we can put our heads together and get everyone aligned. We are respectful of one another. We appreciate one another.

Personal training might include seminars about well being and happiness. Training might be in yoga or meditation. This sort of training supports a person in being at peace in their life. When people are at peace with themselves they are free to be respectful, kind, patient and bring integrity and empowerment to their work. There is much opportunity for the students when the teacher brings a sense of peace and self actualization to the learning environment. There is patience, acceptance and understanding that creates a safe place for students, especially students who may be fearful and who may not have seen much success in the past. A safe environment is important. A safe environment sets a good example.

<u>Let's Imagine some possibilities for students in the public schools.</u>

- 100% Graduation Rate.

- 100% of the Graduates go on to college. That could mean a one year Training Program or a two or three or more year program that would sufficiently train a person to be qualified for a career.

- Cooperative and Kind students-Zero Suspensions/Expulsions.

- Attendance Rate above 98%.

- An On Time Rate that has never been seen before in education.

- All Grades on the Report Cards are "B" or better. Intervention happens as soon as the need arises.

- All students meet the clearly stated criteria for moving on to the next grade level.

Living into what is possible
is exciting!

In boldness, we can see clearly.

Speaking begins the process.

Taking action that aligns with
the possibility is crucial.

Creating the conversation
and then enrolling others
into that possibility,
gets the momentum started.

In our imaginations
we can feel the joy
and the peace.

Can <u>YOU</u>
see the possibility yet?

Life is for us to invent.

It is time to invent our public schools
to be extraordinary.

It is time for Detroit
to be peaceful and prosperous!

<u>Imagine this, now.</u>

Peace

Joy

Happiness

Being Accomplished

Contributing

Responsibility

Forgiveness

Being Complete

The Sock Drawer in Order

A Retirement Plan

Money in the Savings Account

What do you want to add to the list?

Go ahead, add them here.

1. _____

2. _____

3. _____

4. _____

5. _____

Live into your possibilities, commit,
take action and see results.

Pre-Pre-School
Parental Participation

It would greatly benefit the children in the city of Detroit to be in an educational program beginning at birth. It may be a program that starts off by meeting one time a month to give parents guidance and watch the development of the child. It might be a yearly check up and workshop to see where the child is developmentally and help parents to understand the normal developmental stages of a child and how they could encourage their child's development. The development of the child and the ability of the parents to nurture and support their child would determine how often they would need to attend the program. This is a time when children need to be monitored carefully for any developmental delay, issues or giftedness.

Regularly scheduled evaluations will assist parents in getting support where it will be most helpful. Early intervention can potentially have a much greater impact than when it is started at a later time in the child's development. When children show up in the kindergarten or first grade and they are having difficulty functioning, it may finally be discovered that there is a hearing or sight problem or another developmental issue that should have been appropriately addressed long before the child entered the kindergarten. Early placement of children with disabilities will forward their education and create peace around the process.

This is a time when the nutritional needs of the child must be addressed. It is so important for the developing child to be consuming foods that are full of nutrition, not empty calories. Often times a child is behaving inappropriately or appears to be very unhappy and uncooperative, this may be due to an inappropriate diet. Too often this child will be diagnosed with a behavior problem and prescribed drugs to deal with that problem and what really needs to happen is to get the child's diet in good order. These drugs have side effects and we are beginning to see what happens to kids who are on these drugs for long periods of time. Along with good nutrition, parents need to be empowered to be loving and patient, to guide and teach their children, not lose their patience and harm them emotionally or physically.

Support for parents is crucial. Training that supports parents in empowering and nurturing their children is key. When parents have learned disempowering ways to parent, a child's self esteem is often destroyed. There is never a place for hitting a child. Never. Hitting a child only damages the relationship between the parent and the child. Any form of abuse contributes to lowering the self esteem of a child.

Discipline means discipleship, it doesn't mean punish or hit. Punishing or hitting comes from an angry and impatient person and that anger and impatience can be extremely detrimental to a child's development. Discipleship is about teaching and guiding. If a child makes a mistake, he didn't get the lesson, the parents or caregivers did not teach the lesson or did not teach the lesson effectively enough or the child would not have made the mistake. It is the responsibility of parents to keep a child safe. If by chance the child went out into the street, it's not the child's fault. It is the responsibility of the parents to keep the child safe, not hit or punish him because they did not do their job effectively and keep the child out of the street or teach them not to go into the street.

Mistakes are a part of life and we need to teach that to our children. We are human beings, making mistakes is part of being a human being. Patience, understanding and a heartfelt conversation about mistakes will help to guide children to make wise choices in the future. Whenever we can teach the lessons and save the children from suffering, we do that. The alternative to patience and understanding is frightful to children. That fear contributes to who they become as they grow older. Do we want our children to be fearful in life or turn into screaming, impatient and angry adults? They may turn into that if that is the example that is set for them. Patience, understanding and conversation is crucial if we intend to empower our children into being happy and productive citizens.

Parenting is the most important job there is. Excellent parenting is not an innate quality for many. There needs to be effective training. Parents need to understand how to empower their children and build their self-esteem, not disempower or harm them. Courses in what it takes to be a great and responsible parent would be ideal for students in the middle school. These courses may prevent some of the unplanned pregnancies and may have these students thinking twice before they venture into becoming a parent.

Planning for parenthood and getting some training to be an effective parent would be appropriate after prenatal examinations.

Babies have a better chance at being healthy if their parents are healthy. Physical and emotional well being is important. Both parents would greatly benefit from this sort of training. Couples, who are married as well as unwed couples who have a child on the way, who fall into the high needs or at risk category, must be required to participate in a series of parenting classes. These parents to be may not even be a couple or ever plan to marry and they are still the parents and both of them have a responsibility in the matter of raising the child. When parents venture into the most important job they will ever have without effective training, there is a great possibility that some damage will be done. Children get hurt and often times stay hurt for the rest of their lives. That contributes to a population that suffers. The cycle continues.

Pre-Pre-School is crucial for the healthy development of the child. This is a time when parents can create a great beginning for their child. This is when the educational process is started if the child is going to be successful and happy throughout their life. This is also a time for parents to look at the appropriateness of having another child, and especially in the case of the unwed, having sex that may result in having another child. When they see what it takes to raise a child to be healthy and happy, supporting them in being wise about choosing to have another one or not to have another one would be most appropriate at this time. Choosing to have a child comes with a great responsibility. Thoughtfulness is appropriate.

This may be a time when parents need support in career guidance. If they are not on track to be financially responsible for the child, career guidance would be most appropriate at this time. Support and guidance can assist parents in creating a good life for themselves and the child. Support and kindness is important at this time. It takes a village and everyone along the way needs to realize that and contribute support where it is clearly needed. This is not a time to pass the buck and not take responsibility for what we see needs to be put in place for the well being of those we are caring for. There has been much passing of the buck and we can see where that has gotten us.

Pre-School

Pre-School Programs prepare the children for kindergarten. Mandatory Pre-School for kids in Detroit would contribute greatly to the success of the public schools.

The playing, learning and social interaction at that age is so important. When children don't learn those pre-school skills and they show up in kindergarten without the ability to sit in their seat and follow the directions of their teacher, they hold the rest of the students hostage. Everyone suffers in the hostage situation and that begins the "getting behind process." When the little ones do not learn what is required and get passed on to the next grade because they got something, it makes it tough to be in the next grade, tough for everyone, again.

Pre-School is a time when kids are to learn that school is a great place and it's a really good thing to be in school. Parent workshops are important at this time, as well. Pre-School is a gateway to our traditional educational process and when the process is loving and positive the family gets set up for a wonderful educational experience that will go on for many years. Right along with the kids, parents can have fun and learn, as well.

Children need to be evaluated at the end of pre-school to see if they are ready to go into a kindergarten class. It may be appropriate for a child to go to a Level Two Pre-School Environment to catch them up. If a child is disruptive or slow to learn, intervention needs to take place. Parents are a part of that process. Specific criteria needs to be met before a child is permitted into a kindergarten classroom.

Behavior, academics and attendance are all a part of the evaluation process. Parents are an integral part of their child's education and the evaluation process. This is a time for serious evaluation. There may be issues that need to be addressed in a self contained Special Education classroom for the developmentally delayed or the gifted child. With appropriate intervention and support at a young age the child will have a better chance of being educated and graduating with all the requirements and prepared for the next level of training. Early intervention and training for parents is crucial and important for the well being of each person who is participating in this process.

Kindergarten

Required.

No kidding.

Class size should be no more than 17 students. No kidding. The Pre-School Programs must abide by the rules about the class size maximum and we must demand appropriate class sizes for the kindergarten classrooms. It is impossible to do an effective job teaching kindergarteners when there are too many children in the classroom. Too many students, along with students who did not attend pre-school and are not ready to cooperate, makes for a stressful day for everyone.

Kindergarteners need to be loved and nurtured and empowered to express themselves and begin to be responsible citizens. They need to have some fun and be given opportunities to play and do art and sing and exercise. The environment is so important.

At the end of the year, evaluations are made and those who are ready will proceed to the first grade. Students who are not prepared for the first grade need to go to a First Grade Readiness Class. This class would be much smaller, say 6 to10 children. Being in a very small class may be all it takes to move them forward. Maybe even at the end of the first semester some children might be able to be moved into a regular size first grade classroom. Every child is unique. Amazing things can happen in a nurturing environment. The teachers placed in those small sized classrooms need to be very special, patient and empowering teachers.

What are you thinking now?

If we are set up to win,

we will win!

Class Size

This is really important. For decades, the teachers in Detroit have been saying that it is often times very difficult to teach the students when you have large class sizes. Forever, the powers that be have not gotten this. It has been about budgeting and that seems to be the place where the cuts are made. It's just plain absurd. All the research says that appropriate class size is crucial to the success of students. 17 students has been the number so often used when schools really want to educate their children. **This needs to be a priority in Detroit.**

Considering the state of the public schools and their test scores at this time, all elementary and middle school classrooms should have a maximum of 17 students in them. We need to catch the students up to their grade levels. The standardized test scores show that we need to do this, now. Some students are at grade level, many are not.

Down the road, a few years after the test scores become acceptable, the 4th thru 8th grades may be able to up the numbers, for now, they need to be capped at 17 students. No exceptions. If a parent comes to a school to enroll their child and the classroom is at full capacity, they need to find another school where there is room for their child. Accepting students into a full classroom is detrimental and has been the practice for decades. That contributes to the ineffectiveness of the educational process. If parents begin to understand that our schools are getting organized in July, they may see the opportunity that having their child registered by July would be for them. There must be a plan in place for the transient students who may show up at anytime during the school year. In past years we have seen many transient students. In some neighborhoods, the class may look very different at the end of the school year than it looked on the first day of school. Creating classes that are oversize is not an appropriate practice. We then are back to the old way, and we know how that does not work. We want it to work for everyone. The plan needs to be set and worked with integrity. Busing needs to be worked out as well. With a city that is so spread out and with few schools left, we must plan ahead.

High School class size should follow suit. Small class sizes make a difference. High school students need to attend school. Reportedly, attendance can be a big issue in high school. If the class sizes are going to be kept at small numbers serious attendance requirements must be in place. Incentives that students actually appreciate may be the support that is needed in order to get students to be in school where teachers are in place and being paid to teach them.

Class size is extremely important.

Small classes work.

Children need nurturing and attention in order to learn.

This must be a priority.

Elementary School
And Middle School

Elementary and Middle school students need to be in two separate buildings. A middle school environment is a very different environment from an elementary school environment. Mixing the two (PK-8) simply creates an environment where there are too many needs. When there are too many needs, they do not get addressed sufficiently. Elementary students do not need to be exposed to the inappropriate behaviors that are often times exhibited by middle school students, especially during this transition time in Detroit.

When you put students in a building that range from a Pre-School level up to the 8th Grade, there is too much going on. There are elementary school needs and middle school needs and dealing with all of them in one building is simply too much to deal with. It may be appropriate to have two completely separate parts of a building, one part for elementary students and one part for the middle school students, where there is no interaction between the students. There could be a central lunchroom where the students would never interact, simply use the same room at different times. Maybe a central kitchen and two different lunchrooms would be a solution. Ideally, in our shrinking city, it may be appropriate to build Middle Schools next door to Elementary Schools or physically attached yet separate, so that it will be convenient for siblings to attend schools that are geographically close by one another. As we are reinventing our city, this may be a good solution to the problem of being so spread out.

Elementary students need an elementary school environment, one that is for kids, young kids. Elementary students need to be in self contained classrooms where they each have a desk, a home where they can keep their belongings. They need stability and the platoon system that is often used in the public schools in Detroit is set up to make the teacher's life easier and it is very disruptive for elementary age students. Self contained classrooms contribute to a peaceful school environment. In middle school the students are beginning to transition into young adults and there is a lot going on with them, they need their own environment to be working those things out. High school is yet another level for young people who are transitioning into young adulthood. They are three different levels and they all need their own unique environments to grow and transition to the next level.

With a shrinking city, it will take planning to make this happen and the time and money it takes to make this happen will be well worth it.

Attendance

Attendance has not played a prominent role in the scheme of promotional things in the public schools over the past three decades. There is clearly something missing with regard to attendance and a responsibility to maintain a good record. You learn more when you are there; you miss things when you are not there. Good attendance comes from your parents. If it is not a priority of one's parents, one will not learn of its importance, unless someone at school helps that young person get a true understanding of its importance. When students understand the importance of being in school every day, they often times on their own, will do just that and be in school and be on time every day!

Attendance incentives that truly create an incentive to attend school would be appropriate. A conversation with students at each school to find incentives that are desirable may support an incentive program that will potentially work. There needs to be incentives for goals that are reached quarterly, by the semester and by the end of the year. Each student who reaches the goal will need to receive the incentive. Incentives for parents may support the program as well. It can't be a competition where students put in the work to reach the goals and not receive the incentive. If a goal is reached, the student and parents will get the incentives. This is where corporations may be able to step up and be very supportive of the school and good attendance practices. Businesses want employees who have good attendance. This is where is begins. Incentives could be effective positive behavior support.

A 98% attendance rate should be mandatory. Parents must attend workshops that will give them an understanding of the importance of ATTENDANCE if students are not attending school at the required rate. Written excuses must also be mandatory. Notes from a doctor must be brought in by the student when they have been to the doctor. Written excuses with documentation are appropriate. There have been too many years of no written excuses and an acceptance of this irresponsibility. When there is no accountability, things fall apart.

Attendance counts.

Written excuses are a must.

If you miss too many days of school,
you attend in the summer.

If you miss the summer,
you are not promoted.

**If you don't pass
the Exit Skills Test
you are not promoted,
simply attending Summer School
should not get one promoted.**

Homework

Homework has a purpose. That purpose is to help the student to deepen the understanding of a concept so that he really gets it!

Homework supports a student in doing better in school.

It is at the elementary level that children need to learn the importance of completing their homework. If parents are not supporting their elementary age children in being responsible about completing and turning in their homework they do not develop good homework habits. When they get into Middle and High School passing with a "C" grade or better may become difficult because homework is such an integral part of their grades. Homework is also about practicing responsibility and consciousness. If these two things are practiced there is a much greater chance for success in the future.

Parents must check the book bags of elementary school children every night for homework and communication from the teacher or the school. Parents need to know the Homework Policy of their child's class/

teacher. Parents need to be in communication with the teacher on a regular basis. If there is any problem going on with the child, Progress Reports are a must, Daily or Weekly, returned with a parent's signature the day after it was sent home.

If a child is not bringing in their Homework, parents must attend Homework Workshops to assist them in understanding the importance of homework and developing the good habits of completing it and turning it in by when it is due, if not before the due date! Doing homework is not an option, it is a requirement.

Homework is an opportunity for parents to see what their kids are up to in school! People who choose to have children need to understand that children are a responsibility and they need to be tended to. Support is important and necessary. We must support parents in nurturing their children. This is a key component if we expect to be successful in educating their children.

Parents must check
book bags nightly.

Parents must look for homework and
other communication
from the teacher or the school.

Parents must know the
Homework Policy.

If the homework isn't being turned in,
mandatory parental participation
in the Homework Workshop is required.

Continued parental training
must take place
until the homework is returned regularly.

Regularly is decided by the teacher
and put in writing
for all to be clear about.

Accountability
by parents and students and teachers
is necessary.

Blocks To Learning

Think about it, if you are attempting to learn something and you are distracted by something you are worried about, something that you really need to be tending to, or there is noise (in your head or your environment) or fear, it is difficult to learn. This is the case with people of any age. When a child is having difficulty learning, there is something in the way of that child's ability to grasp the concept or do what he is being requested to do. There are a number of things that get in the way of a child's ability to learn.

If a child who is diagnosed with autism gets quick and effective interventions, miraculous things can happen. Effective intervention has the potential to change the course that a child is on and is an important part of the educational process, if we are going to be successful at educating our children. I do not attempt to discuss in depth all of the possible issues that may be the cause of a learning disability here and now. I will present some of what my experience says may be happening with regard to a child's inability to learn at a normal pace.

Picture in your mind a loved and nurtured child who has all of his basic needs met. He has a loving mother and father and loving grandparents. He is fed and kept warm enough in the winter and cool enough in the summer. He has toys and watches appropriate TV and plays appropriate games. The nurtured child is told that he's great and can be and do anything he sets his mind to be and do. The nurtured child has a clear head and few, if any, worries or concerns to occupy his mind as the school day goes on. This child is set up to be able to learn and usually does learn what is presented to him. This child does well in school and succeeds in life to carry on the tradition of success with the next generation of his family.

Then we have children who have distractions that get in the way of learning. Take for instance a child who;

1) has one parent, maybe never knew or doesn't see the other parent, or it's a grandparent or an aunt or an uncle or a great aunt or a great uncle or a foster parent who is raising him, they may be loving and nurturing or not. When a child does not have both of his parents to support and nurture him, the circumstances that revolve around this issue may cause a distraction for the child.

2) has a parent/guardian who did not plan for the child and is struggling financially or in other ways that may create stress for the child.

3) has a parent/guardian who is using drugs or alcohol and is not there (present and caring) for the child or placing the child in a dangerous situation.

4) has a parent(s)/guardian who may move every few months for any number of reasons. When they can't manage getting the rent paid, the landlord sold the house or lost the house in foreclosure, there is a case of domestic abuse or the house burned down, it creates disruption and insecurity. Moving from one school to another is very hard on a child's capacity to learn, they need to orient themselves to the new environment, the house, the school, the teacher, the students, etc., it's a lot for the mind to process. There is only so much capacity for learning and the school work is usually not the priority.

5) has a parent who is illiterate and unable to assist the child with

homework or who may even have their own issues about school and is unwilling to even be with the child about anything associated with the school.

6) has a parent who is not happy, therefore unable to nurture and support the child.

7) has a parent who has serious mental problems from drug use, depression or even their own childhood issues that were never resolved.

8) has a parent with a serious temper problem and may be very violent.

9) has a parent who believes that hitting a child with a belt or an extension cord to punish the child is appropriate, one who believes in punishment rather than support, understanding and consequences.

10) has a parent who may not be providing the child with a bed or nutritious food or a place to call his own to keep his belongings and do his homework.

11) has a parent who cannot provide a clean uniform for the child to wear to school each day.

12) has a parent who cannot get the child to school on time and/or the child misses many days of school due to a variety of reasons: the car isn't working, the student needed to stay home and babysit a sibling because mom had to go to work or they don't have warm enough outer clothing to venture out into the cold.

13) has a parent who has no desire to be in communication with the school or the child's teacher, sometimes after repeated requests for a parent to come to school and find out what he can do to help his child.

The list could go on. I think you are getting the picture of neglect, a lack skills on behalf of the parent(s) or possibly fear and avoidance. There is a clear correlation between who parents are being and the success of their child. Once in a while there are little miracles that happen regardless of the parenting situation. Generally speaking, it is who the parents are being that contribute majorly to the ability of the child to learn and be successful in life. Supporting and nurturing the parents of the struggling students in the public schools is a big part of the plan for success in Detroit.

Good parenting skills
are crucial to the success of children.

Parenting is not an innate skill for many,
support and training are necessary.

Offering parents workshops to enhance their
personal well being will support them
in being good parents.

It's best when both parents of a child
are participating in the child's life.
Sometimes that may not be possible.
If both parents are not there, the child needs to
understand that there are circumstances that
keep the other parent away.

Authenticity and communication
are key factors to success.

Middle School aged students
need to be prepared
for parenting.

The roles and responsibilities
of a parent,
need to be a part of
the Home and Family Living Curriculum
at the Middle School Level.

Having students understand
the sacredness of making a child
must be a priority
for middle school students.
Learning about
all the responsibilities,
including the financial and emotional aspects,
are important lessons
for every student
to get a deep understanding about.

Parental Support And Training
Must Be Mandatory
If A Child Is Not Meeting
The Standards
Set By The District

The student's learning must be measured
quarterly, so that when an intervention is
needed it happens immediately.

Too many children have slipped through
the cracks with regard to the needed
interventions. Individual support
will potentially keep them on track so that
they may be promoted to the next grade.

If a child is not meeting the criteria
with regard to:
Attendance, Behavior and Academics,
it must be mandatory that parents participate
in workshops that will support them
in supporting their children
in being successful.

When parents work with teachers
and the school,
children have a greater opportunity to learn
and be successful in life.

If parents are lacking in good parenting skills and that is manifesting itself in children who have poor attendance, are late for school, have behavior problems or are having difficulty learning, parents need to step up and accept the help that is being offered to them. The support is for them, to help them assist their child(ren). All parents want their children to succeed and be happy. Sometimes it is difficult for parents to understand that the teachers and the school district want to help them to help their children. Teachers understand that parents get frustrated with their children and may not know what to do to help them. The teachers and parents are partners in the educational process. When parents have the tools and skills, they can be true partners!

When parents are happy with themselves and confident in their abilities, their children have a much greater chance at succeeding in school and in life. We want happy parents as partners.

Parents truly want their children
to be successful in life.

It is time for all parents
to understand
how to empower
their children.

If we want to be good at something,
we get support and training.

Parenting
is the most important job
that anyone will ever have.

When children are struggling,
parents are in need of support.

It is time for transformation to take place.

Realizing that things
could be really fabulous
and there really could be
Peace on Earth,
and peace within,
is a beginning for transformation.

Transformation is a process.

Imagining can sometimes be scary,
because one must be
bold to imagine.

Boldness brings out fear sometimes.

It is in the boldness
that ingenuity materializes.

When we be around others who are
bold in their thinking,
it's easier to be bold and ingenuity
becomes a familiar thing.

What can you imagine?

What is possible for you in your life?

Go ahead, be bold.

Imagine.

Believe.

Appropriately Behaved Students
Are Necessary If The Teachers Are Going To Be Able To Educate The Students

In most educational settings there is a teacher and students and they are in a classroom. The teacher has a plan of action, curriculum, etc., and the students come to learn what the teacher is offering. When students show up with issues that distract them and they become disruptive, the learning process is delayed. This type of disruption has been taking place for over three decades. Inappropriate behavior and disrespectful attitudes have been huge contributing factors to why we stand where we do in Detroit today.

There must be a plan in place to address the inappropriately behaved, disruptive students. Holding the well behaved and cooperative students hostage is presently and has been for many years a big deterrent to the learning process in the public schools. If the class sizes become smaller, this issue of the inappropriately behaved is lessened and could contribute greatly to potentially disappearing the problem. We have not set ourselves up to win, we have compounded the problems. We have not created the peace in our classrooms that is necessary if we are to succeed. The size of the class makes an incredible difference in the climate of the classroom and an observer would instantly see that with fewer students in the classroom there is a peace amidst the classroom that calms the souls and opens up an opportunity for learning to take place. Some students bring a lot of activity into the classroom and when there are lots of students interacting with lots of other students it gets exponentially noisy and the interactions can become argumentative. Sometimes all it takes is one student who brings many issues with him into the classroom and that may create a volatile situation.

Inappropriately behaved students and not having a plan to effectively work with them to change their behavior is a reason so many teachers have gotten out of teaching in the public schools, either they went to another district or simply retired due to exhaustion or an unwillingness to be so disrespected by one more student. These students are not happy and we have failed them by not setting ourselves up to win. We have not created learning environments that address the needs of our students. They are not to be blamed. They are victims and then we become their victims. It is time for a change.

During this transition time, as everyone is getting on board with smaller class sizes and positive behavior support is becoming a big part of the culture, teachers need the opportunity to have the disruptive students removed from their classrooms. When there is not a plan for this, the disruptive and disrespectful students all know that and the teacher is powerless to carry on in the classroom. The disruptive students need support, it is clear that they are a request for support. When a student is removed from a classroom for being disruptive he needs to get that support as soon as the support can be offered to him. Parents need to be brought in for consultation. Repeat offenders (students with 3 suspensions) need a plan outside the regular school setting. An alternative school setting may be very appropriate for the student who repeatedly disrupts a classroom. When students repeatedly disrupt we must intervene by removing the student from the regular school setting so that the rest of the students can carry on with their educations. The repeat offender needs serious support and intervention that is not available in a regular school setting. Kids like this need support every morning. They need to sit down with a supportive coach and set their day up. They need to be in an environment that is not going to set them off. They need to be in an environment with patient and nurturing people who are not going to confront them. They need love, patience and understanding.

The teachers also need support and having a disruptive student removed from the classroom would finally begin to have students realize that inappropriate and disrespectful behavior is not acceptable and there are consequences. The inability of teachers to be in control of the classroom has contributed hugely to the breakdown of the school district and the city. If this is not addressed we will not see a transformation, we will continue to witness the decline, the poverty, the crime, the depression and everything else that goes along with that, not to mention the potential for gun violence.

Positive behavior support
is an effective way of
addressing the inappropriately behaved student.

Catching students doing something right
will change the way they feel about themselves.

Often times the disrupter
only wants attention
and to that point
only knows how to get it
by doing something wrong
instead of doing something right.

If we can ignore the small distractions,
look for the good stuff
and acknowledge it,
we will be assisting that child into realizing
that he is extraordinary!

Some kids need more support than others.

If a child understands that his teachers
are his coaches,
and coaches only want the players
to win and be really great at what they do,
they can be open to being coached.

Teachers need to let children know
that they are the coach,
not the criticizers, the meanies
or the one to avoid.

Redirecting is a process that is gentler
than telling a child that he is
doing something wrong.

Praising and acknowledging are nurturing
and like a flower
that gets water and sunshine, it blooms,
the child will bloom
when he is acknowledged and praised!

Let me acknowledge that many of the ideas
mentioned here about praising, redirecting,
ignoring and criticizing come from the incredible
book, "Whale Done," by Ken Blanchard, Thad
Lacinak, Chuck Tompkins and Jim Ballard.

Every staff member in the public schools
must be on board with
<u>Positive Behavior Support</u>.

Praising
Redirecting
Acknowledging
Patience
Nurturing
Loving Attitude
Loving Tone
Understanding
Respecting
Listening, really listening
Smiling
Being Pleasant
Being Kind

If we are all being this list of ways to be
we will create peace and learning will
be taking place.

Qualities that we would like to see in our students include;

1. Understanding why we have procedures that are to be followed and the ability to follow them.

2. An understanding that cooperation works for everyone.

3. A disciplined work ethic and an understanding for why that is good.

4. Being Responsible.

5. Being Kind.

6. Excellent Attendance Ethic.

7. Working smart and with ease.

8. Confidence with respectful humility.

9. Being coachable and the ability to listen to themselves when it comes to figuring out who's a coach and who's not a coach and who's to be trusted and who's not to be trusted.

10. Being inventive.

A well developed Character Education Foundation

at the Elementary Level will set
the Middle School up
with a cooperative learning environment
with much opportunity for academic success.
District wide lessons on
Integrity, Kindness, Respect,
Forgiveness, Thankfulness, Courage,
Responsibility, Confidence, Humility
and Pride in taking care of one's environment
will support students
in taking on those qualities.
These lessons must be taught with
heart and soul in order for students
to BE these qualities.
The young students can
use these words in sentences
and the older students
might create stories or even plays/videos
about these character traits.
Thoughtful discussion
with a purpose
could have a student
believe that they are that quality.

Can you imagine what the world would be like if
everyone would BE these qualities?

When the distraction of
inappropriately behaved students is diminished,
students can learn,
students get excited about learning
and they can begin to take full responsibility
for their lives.

They see the reasoning behind wise choices.
They understand why they are in school.

School becomes an opportunity,
it is no longer about suffering and hard work.

It is a place to work smart.

When the light bulb turns on,
the smiling sets in!!!

Promotion From
One Grade To The Next

Promotion with integrity will create intervention strategies like never before in the past. Social Promotion has been a practice in the public schools for many years. It is time for everyone to know the clearly stated criteria necessary for promotion to the next grade level. Children must know the exit skills; they must be prepared for the next grade level. When children are passed onto the next grade and they are not prepared, they suffer and fall further behind and the behavior problems occur even more often.

Clearly stated criteria must be in writing for all to see and know regarding promotion to the next grade level.

Parents need to be clear about what their child will need to learn in order to be promoted to the next grade level.

Quarterly evaluations need to be taking place.

Interventions must be put in place
immediately, where there are deficits.

Parents will need to be a part
of all of this.

We cannot leave one child behind
on this educational journey.

If we were going on a trip
across the desert
we would want to make sure
that everyone had a canteen of water,
in other words,
they were prepared to take care of themselves.
We want everyone to have
a canteen of water.
The goal is personal responsibility
and a joyful and peaceful life for all.

Volunteerism

Middle School students need to get with volunteerism. Getting outside of themselves and assisting others is a very good practice.

High School students need to understand the importance of giving of themselves for the good of humankind. It is satisfying to contribute.

Volunteering requirements for promotion need to be in place for both Middle and High School students.

At each school a team needs to assess what the school needs to get accomplished. When the needs list is compiled, the students sign up to volunteer and get the tasks completed. It is a great way to get some things accomplished at each school and provide volunteer requirement opportunities for the students. This will also provide an opportunity for students to take pride in contributing to the well being of their environment. Volunteering outside of school is a great practice as well.

Ideas . . . .

Taking care of the school yard.

Landscaping.

Keeping the halls clean.

Making sure the lavatories stay clean.

Painting.

Student Council.

Other invented projects where there is a need.

What Is Missing In Detroit That Needs To Be Addressed?

Really, what is missing?
What needs to be put in place?
What needs attention?

We need to look at what is going on in this city to know what is missing. What is going on in this city?

There is a lot going on that I have not seen or have not been exposed to. I will address what stood out for me as I worked in this city and drove through many parts of this city. This is what I see.

First of all, there are lots of great
things going on in this city.
That is so extraordinary!
What I am looking at here are
the things that are missing by
stating something that is
not being tended to.

Attention is missing in the arenas
that are listed.

These are the things that stand out to the
observer as they drive through Detroit.

**Trash, so much trash in
so many places.**

Broken down buildings.

Piles of old discarded tires.

Unkempt property.

Broken down everything.

**Big and small piles of junk,
everywhere.**

Graffiti.

Burned out and
falling down buildings.

Poorly maintained everything,
streets, sidewalks, curbs,
fields, etc.

Signage that
clutters up the environment.

People think they can put a sign
up anywhere they please.

Obesity.

Many poor health issues.

People who are not well.

Poverty.

Stealing cars.

Stealing other things.

Thieves using guns.

Violence.

Lots of drug use, legal and illegal.

Drug related crimes.

Other crime.

Girls and women having children
without a plan to take care of
them emotionally or financially.

Many generations of welfare.
Resignation that creates welfare
as the only solution.

This is what is going on in much of Detroit.

For years the public schools have been
attempting to educate the children.
Some of them got a pretty good education!
Some of them did not.

Many issues at hand, are not being addressed.

Addressing the needs of the population
is crucial, if we would like to be successful with every
student. It is time to address the needs of
each and every student.

What Is Needed?
Where do we pay our attention?

Education.

When there is a problem, we look for a solution.

It is simple.

Education.

We need to set up an educational program
that is effectively and efficiently managed.

We need to address the issues at hand.

Patience, Love and Understanding
are all a part of the plan.

Small classes
will make the difference.

**Classes that are too large will continue
to sabotage any possibility
of transformation.**

It is time to address the true needs of the
City of Detroit.

A Plan Of Action.

Organization, planning ahead,
no more, by the seat of our pants planning
in a frantic state of upset.

Planning.

Setting up a calendar, in advance . . . .
Planning.

More Planning.

Peace is the state of Being
that is desired as we work
to create the Peace for all.

What is Missing?

<u>Integrity</u>
<u>Values</u>
<u>Responsibility</u>
<u>True Peace</u>
<u>Education</u>
<u>Community</u>
<u>Confidence</u>
<u>Faith</u>
<u>Joy</u>
<u>Possibility</u>
<u>Opportunity</u>
<u>Fun</u>
<u>Pride</u>
<u>Love</u>
<u>Happiness</u>
<u>Parental Participation</u>

Fortunately, we do see some of the above.
We need to see that everywhere,
not just occasionally.
Those ideas, ways of being need
to live in our existence.
Take Integrity for example, you can't just
think about having that on occasion.
When we BE Integrity, we live free.
Can you imagine if everyone is being
integrity and free!
Some think about how much they can get
away with, if no one is looking.
We are one race, the human race.
We live together on this planet.
When we come together and work together
like we are all related, we will create peace.
Detroit will be a happy place.
We are one.

BE Integrity.

Watch the transformation appear
before your eyes.

Curriculum
For All Levels:
The Basic Three

<u>Art</u>
<u>Music</u>
<u>Physical Education</u>

In the public schools
there are some
excellent educational
programs in place.
We need to keep those in place
and add some things to the
curriculum that have been taken
out over the years, during the
falling down of Detroit.

A curriculum that includes Art, Music and
Physical Education is such an opportunity for
the public schools. To quote a bumper sticker,
"You gotta have ART." When children are
given the opportunity to express themselves by
creating art they are becoming the inventors of
our future. When we use the part of the brain

that invents, it gets stronger. If we do not use that part of the brain, it is weakened. When we use our imaginations it helps us to create a brain that can solve problems and come up with solutions in all areas of our lives. If it is not given the opportunity to be flexed and worked, it will not develop. Creative thinking, using one's imagination, is necessary for the species and for inventing a life that one desires to live. Art can be lots of fun for kids (and adults), too. It can be pleasurable, satisfying, relaxing and a break from the work that the other side of the brain is doing. Balancing the brain is healthy.

And Music, seriously, it is such a missing in the curriculum. Kids need to sing and learn about Music and Motown. Music can be so powerful and relaxing and moving. Can you imagine a world without music? We so need to support our children in being educated about music. Sadly, when children are not exposed to the classics and genres other than the contemporary music of the day, they are missing so much. Cutting music from the curriculum is like cutting off the oxygen in a classroom, a bad idea. The attitude is, that music is not a necessary part of life or the curriculum. Some exposure every year through the 8th grade will greatly contribute to the well being of the students. Music may be a pathway to success and prosperity in a student's life. If we do not teach our children about music on a regular basis it will continue to be a tragedy.

Our children need Physical Education, taught by a Physical Education Teacher who really knows what a Physical Education Curriculum is all about. Kids need to exercise and learn about leisure activities and have some fun doing physical things. This will contribute greatly to eliminating the obesity problem in this city. Physical Education has not been a priority in many schools for many years. We all know that physical activity is crucial to our health and well being.

Each of these areas has so much to offer the children who are our future. Imagining a world without art or music or physical education creates emptiness, sadness, a big missing. When people understand and imagine the impact that not being educated in these areas will have on the future generations, they will see the need to have them in the curriculum, throughout their K-12 years.

Elementary students need exposure to Art, Music and Physical Education throughout their elementary school years.

Middle School students also need a plan throughout the middle school years that will give them some exposure each year in the areas of Art, Music and Physical Education.

Required Exit Skills for each grade level in these subjects will contribute to a well rounded student. They are all viable Career Pathways that are being taken away from students who may not fit into an "academic" Career Pathway.

Library/Media/Computer is
important for students at every
level to get an understanding
of the technology of today.
Criteria for promotion regarding
computer understanding
needs to be in the
Required Exit Skills.
Scheduling these courses for all
students is necessary.

Our High Schools in Detroit must
offer a well rounded curriculum.
The Visual Arts, Music and Physical
Education all need to be offered and
there needs to be some Requirements
associated with these three
areas as well.

A Conversation
For a
Home and Family Living
Curriculum

If we look at what is missing
it is clear that we need to
create wellness in this city.

The disorder happens out of
not being peaceful.

The disorder happens when people
are depressed
and people do not have a sense
of who they really are.

When there are generations of
families that are dysfunctional,
societies fall apart, disappear and
live lives that are full of suffering.

Sadly, we have perpetuated the
problem by enabling girls and women
to have children with absolutely no
plan to take care of them, other than
the plan that society's responsible
people can take care of them and
their children.

There are too many cases
of girls and women
who continue to have children
with no plan to care for them.
There is much instability.

This creates a very stressful
situation for many.

This may very well be the crux of
our problem here in Detroit.

Poverty.

Poverty can be a vicious cycle.

When this issue of poverty is
addressed we will have a chance
at Detroit's complete turnaround.

We can't have poverty and violence
holding this city's greatness hostage
any longer.

That is what is happening.

Everything that is missing,
everything that is a request for
repair stems from this poverty.

Not everyone who is poor
with regards to their money
is contributing to our problems
in Detroit, generally speaking it is
directly related to our issues at hand.

Depression and sadness
lead to drug use/abuse
and very often in that madness,
is the making of a child(ren).

Depression and sadness often times
come with generational poverty.

This is not a child issue,
this is a family issue.

Many families are in need of support.

Before our children have any more
children, we need to intervene.

The interventions need to be
made in the areas of,

1. Loving One's Self
2. Seeing Possibilities for a Great Life
3. Understanding what a Career is
4. Understanding what Welfare is

5. Understanding what taking full responsibility for one's life really means
6. Understanding the <u>sacredness</u> of having sex
7. Understanding why abstinence is necessary
8. Living a Great and Responsible Life with the benefits that come with that way of living.

The intervention is to break the cycle of poverty and irresponsibility.

The intervention is to create lives filled with joy and happiness.

Who doesn't want that for everyone?

No one likes to see people living in sadness.

No one likes to see people struggle.

It is time that we make the changes
that will make the difference.

It is time for peace.

IT IS TIME.

It is time to end the suffering in Detroit.

It is time for Detroit to be great again!

So, what do we do?
Educate.

Middle School Curriculum

I do not write the Curriculum here. I offer up an outline as to what I see is necessary in order to intervene and create the possibility for Detroit to emerge once again as the great city she once was.

10 Week Quarters
6th Grade

1. Human Sexuality/Abstinence/Well Being/Responsibility
2. Nutrition and Health/Foods and Healthy Cooking
3. Money (A Full Curriculum for the Middle School Years)
4. Career Guidance (Using Michigan's Career Pathways)
   Scholarship opportunities begin in Middle School

7th Grade

1. Human Sexuality/Relationships/ Marriage/Responsibility
2. Nutrition and Health/Cardio/Weights/ Yoga/Meditation/Drug Use and Abuse
3. Money
4. Career Guidance/Michigan's Pathways/ Income

8th Grade

1. Human Sexuality/Babies and what it's really like to care for one
2. Home Environment/Caring for One's Home/Pride in the Planet's Environment/Visual Peace
3. Money
4. Career Guidance/Preparing for High School/Career Exploration

This is not suggested as an Elective Curriculum. This must be required in order for a student to be promoted to the next grade. Students must pass these courses with a "B" grade. Students need to truly understand the content of these courses. This is addressing the "What's Missing," that we need to put in, that will make the change, that will contribute to the recovery of our city.

You may ask, these things are not being taught in the schools at this time? Some of it may be happening here and there. It is not happening across the board, in every Middle School.

Do you think that this makes sense? If you do, go tell the leadership what you think. Encourage them to get this curriculum going as soon as possible.

High School Curriculum

We need to keep the momentum going and make sure that these topics are addressed in the curriculum at the high school level. Some topics can be addressed in Core Curriculum Courses. However they are incorporated makes little difference, we need to make sure that they do not forget what they have already learned with regard to:

Human Sexuality/Abstinence

Nutrition and Health

Money Responsibility/ Consciousness

Career Guidance/Possibilities

Student's need Counselors who have the time to counsel them and guide them and support them in creating fabulous lives for themselves! A schedule needs to be set up in August and every student needs to visit his counselor each semester for a minimum of one class period. Counselors need to guide students and be their champion for whatever it is they want to invent for themselves.

Counselors need to be realistic at this level. There are certain criteria that must be met if one intends to be a doctor or a professional basketball player. This is a get real time. Dreams are to be encouraged and supported as well. This is where the guidance comes in. In order to realize the dreams, there are actions that need to take place. Being in action is crucial for the dream to be realized.

Students who are exposed to a variety of careers have their eyes opened to opportunities. If they understand what a Career Pathway is, they can explore their fields of interest. When they discover what they are good at they can look down the pathway related to what they have already shown success in. A well equipped Career Guidance Center would be an asset for any school.

When there is a good foundation of reality and support, our students can soar to great heights and become successful and happy in life!

Education is the key.

The Budget

All this will take having
a Budgeted Plan.

This will take wise spending.

This will take being conservative.

This will take ingenuity.

This will take being respectful to
everyone who is involved.

A plan like this will need a few years
to really take effect.

We must all bring patience, love and
respect to the profession of teaching.

This may be a time to organize the
volunteers, organize the school
support teams, and do what it is
going to take to transform this
school district and this city.

Some Other Issues

Clean the buildings.
Check the air and water quality.
Get the stuff out of the
closets and cupboards
that has been there for decades.

Fix the broken down buildings
that will remain
in the midst of the shrinking district.

Have bathrooms with toilets that
work with doors for some privacy
and sinks that work.

Have security cameras
everywhere it is appropriate
and security guards watching 24/7
from a central location,
with the ability to dispatch police
as soon as something suspicious
is detected.

Get Green

Many of us have gradually begun to go with more earth friendly ways; it is time that the public schools get on board and do the same.

First, Recycling must be incorporated
into <u>every</u> school's plan.
We need to recycle the Styrofoam,
etc., from the lunchroom and any and
all paper that is discarded.
There are Green School Guidelines
that show the way to
ecological correctness.

Going Organic with the Lawn Care is
only appropriate considering all the
bad effects of the pesticides, etc.

Any Green Technology needs to begin
being a part of the public schools.
Hot Water Heaters.
Solar Panels.
Efficient Heaters.

Alternative light bulbs.
to name a few . . . .

The students and teachers at the
Randolph Career and Technical
Center or other high schools can
work with the district on this!

We need to seek out the professionals
in this arena and step up and get
with the program, don't sit around
on our outdated ways.

School Yard Landscaping/Care

This is such a wonderful opportunity to teach Entrepreneurial Skills as well as simply supporting students in understanding how to make their yard look really great and take pride in maintaining it!

Landscaping Corp Plan of Action

Every High School could have a team of students who are enrolled in a course on Being an Entrepreneur. In the class, students will learn about how to run a business and learn some landscaping skills as well. Another perk would be that they may realize that it is satisfying work and those in the course would be able to put those skills to work at their own homes, now and in the future.

Some thoughts related to this Plan of Action

We will need a strong leader to set this program up for all the High Schools.

Follow through is important, those leading at the schools need to run a tight ship and have integrity about getting things accomplished.

This Team would ultimately take care of all the Middle Schools and Elementary Schools that are geographically close by.

Teams at the Middle Schools and Elementary Schools could assist the High School Teams at their schools.

A program like this can potentially save the district money and probably, more importantly, instill a sense of pride in one's property.

Landscaping Design can be incorporated into the course.

All sorts of Horticulture Lessons could be taught.

We could even enroll some Landscaping Companies to possibly assist with this Project. It could be an opportunity for contribution to the schools and the City of Detroit for Landscaping Companies.
(A Positive Partnership)

Snow removal could also be taken care of,
if the leader of this project thinks big and
doesn't let anything get in his way
of accomplishing the amazing!
At least the shoveling part
of the snow removal!

The teams might even turn out
summer teams that earn some income!
They can create their own companies
with a Logo and A Business Plan for a Loan
so they can buy some equipment
to do the work!

The Business Plans could be for any sort of
business the students are interested in.

Detroit is waiting for them.

Who's Your School?

Every school could have a Team of Volunteers who are there to assist in (most) any way needed.

This Team (background checked) would be like a Board of Directors.

They could throw a family community dinner.

They could supervise on the playground at lunchtime.

They could donate money.

They could be Career Speakers.

They could help with the maintenance of the building.

We'd have to have a Director and Committee Heads for things to be orderly and efficient.

This needs to be set up as a help to the Administration of a school, not be more work or a hindrance.

Everyone could wear shirts and hats stating that they are part of the Detroit School Team!

What fun, contributing and making a difference in Detroit!

Are you feeling it? Are you smiling?

Every Child Needs The Opportunity To Play Sports

Neighborhood Sports make
participation possible.

Transportation is a problem
with some kids.

There are Recreation Centers
in Detroit.
Full out programs need to be going
on at every Recreation Center.

This is another opportunity
to contribute.
Create a program, be it in golf
or little league or soccer or even
exercise and figure out how you can
make it become a reality!

Maybe you want to get kids on their
bikes, invent a schedule and
meet up with the kids.
Maybe you could bring the bikes!

All this signing up doesn't have to be
for the rest of your life, just a season,
at your own pace!

You know they will love it and you,
for your contribution to them!!!

Are you enrolled yet?

How much fun could it be!

Investigate the opportunities, think big and
don't let anything get in your way of making
incredible things happen!

This is a city waiting to happen.
BE in action.
Disrupt the waiting with your love and energy
and kindness and creativity.
Eventually there will be a breakthrough.

Integrity

Integrity is a way of Being.

Let us all Be Integrity.

The American Heritage Dictionary of the
English Language defines integrity as;

1. Rigid adherence to a code of behavior;
   probity
2. The state of being unimpaired; soundness
3. Completeness; unity

Being Integrity is something we
practice Being.

The more we practice, the better we get.

There is such a freedom that is created
in Integrity.
In that freedom there is much peace.

Then we can smile.

Then come the tears
of being complete and satisfied.

Peace is with us.

Just What Is Possible?

Every Detroiter
being kind to one another.

Responsibility.

No more violence.

No more killing people.

No more stealing.

No more stealing at gun point.

Maintenance of all property.

Not a piece of trash on the ground.

All the old and broken down, gone.

No more graffiti.

No more piles of old tires.

A city who recycles, seriously.

Lots more trees!

Beautiful landscaping.

Lots (more) of really cool restaurants!

Lots of fun!

A new title, Detroit; Friendly Capital
of the Planet!

OK

Add yours here,
go ahead, have some fun of your own.

Where Will You Play?

What action will you take that will contribute
to creating peace, prosperity
and joy in Detroit?

Adopt a school?

Plant trees?

Help with a Literacy Program?

Create a company
that creates jobs for Detroiters?

Come on down.

Be a part
of the change.

Make a difference.

Have some fun!

Smile!

I thank God,
for being with me
through all my years
working in Detroit.

I thank Him
for guiding my hand
as I wrote these ideas down
to share with you.

This is about love and peace.

I thank God
for all he has blessed me with.

I thank God for forgiveness.

I thank God for Peace.

True Peace.

Dear Lord God in Heaven,

We put Detroit in your hands.

We pray for her Peace.

We pray for her Prosperity.

**We pray for her return
to being the Great City
that she once was,
who offers opportunity and
happiness to her people.**

We put her in your hands, Lord.

**In Jesus' name,
Amen**

If you

see an opportunity,

please take action.

You

can do this.

Show your love.